One Page At A Time:

Getting Through College With ADHD

Phill Pappas

ISBN: 0615523722
ISBN-13: 978-0615523729

Cover design by Alex Pappas

For my family

I have never been welcome at a more entertaining dinner table than our own

"Close the gate."

Contents

Home

School

Life

First introduction

I started writing this book in the summer of 2010. My idea was to sit down and write something honest, useful, and to the point. I have not included every detail of my life in this book. I have written about what helped me get through college.

Second introduction

I believe this book can be helpful even if you don't have ADHD, and you aren't in college.

People take different paths coming out of high school, and I don't think there is a right or wrong, it's more what works for you and what doesn't. Learning a trade works for some. Working fulltime satisfies the needs in others. Some people continue on in the educational system. And others take yet a different path. I truly believe each of these choices has its own merit, and that each of these choices can make different people happy. This book does not argue for or against secondary education. I am simply sharing my thoughts and experiences.

Third introduction: you don't have to read this one

Really, you don't. Feel free to skip to any section. I hate reading introductions.[1]

I have ADHD. And, I'm guessing that you, your lover, your child, or your love child, has ADHD as well. Otherwise, you wouldn't be reading this, would you?

This book is the culmination of 12 years of techniques, strategies, school and life experiences, and any other advice or wisdom that I have found helpful in dealing with ADHD.

Read this book any way you want to. If you want to pick it up and read it straight through, do it. If you want to pick it up every once in a while, so be it. The point is to take one thing at a time, and apply it to your life. Make one change at a time, if you believe it could help.

Everything you will read here has somehow helped me, either by doing it or just knowing it. My hope is for you to come away with an understanding of what can be done to alter the ways that you operate, to create positive change.

---

1 And that's why I just wrote three of them.

Back in the day

In my youth, my dad walked me to elementary school every day. Each morning, before I entered the building, he would say, "Remember, if you focus you can be a leader." I would say something to the effect, "I'll do my best, pops." By the time I walked through the red doors of the school, however, these sage words would be filed somewhere in my mental rolodex under, "Blah blah blah, blah blah blah blah."

It's not that I didn't care about his advice – at this age, pops was the wisest person I knew. It's just that while he was speaking, I was thinking about the bird that just flew by, my friend Matt who just walked into school, how the car parked outside was missing a hubcap, and that the broken bottle by the curb could be used as a weapon if I was suddenly mugged.

At school, my favorite parts of the day were recess, snack time, lunch, post-lunch recess, and after-school care. When mom or dad picked me up, around five-o-clock, my clothes were dirty, I was yapping up a storm, and a teacher would speak to them about something I did. Overall, it was another good day at school.

This system work well for a while, until people started expecting things from me.

These infidels expected homework to be turned in, musical instruments to be practiced, planners to be written in, a hand to be raised before speaking, manners to be followed, actions to be thought through, and consequences to be thought of. Bullshit, I know, and it only got worse.

I spent the majority of middle school and high school doing everything I could to get by. I was too tired to pay attention in my first two classes. Sometimes, I'd fall asleep. Later in the day, I had too much energy to stay in my seat.

I only read two books in high school, "The Catcher in the Rye" and "The Odyssey," so I found other ways to get information. I'd talk with people about the books, ask open-ended questions in class, take notes when I could, and, in general, bullshit or joke my way out of any formidable situation.

When I got to college, however, there was simply too much learning to do, and I needed to change my ways. I had to learn to operate at a much higher level than I had ever before, both as a student and as a person. It took me six-and-a-half years to graduate college, and, using the tricks I had learned, I four pointed every class of the second semester of my super senior year.

What this book is and what it is not

This book is a tool. I want you to understand what you can do to be more successful. I want you to walk away with the feeling that adapting is crucial and giving up is not an option. I want you to try things out. If you think something might work for you, give it a shot. I have read too many articles and heard too many lectures on ADHD that tell you what you shouldn't do.

"Don't procrastinate," the Ph.D. speaker says, "Procrastination is bad." And then they keep speaking for an hour-and-a-half, and their lecture is the epitome of boredom. This type of advice makes me want to shove their useless PowerPoint lecture up their ego-filled rectum. It's useless because it fails to capture what we need to hear, and how we need to hear it. Their message is dead before the presentation starts. They are not speaking for us. And that is what I want to accomplish here.

Everything that you read here will be direct, unless I go on a tangent about cavemen or ninjas. For this, I apologize in advance.[1]

The goal is to pass on the techniques and skills that I have learned. The goal is not to simply state the obvious, and then act like I just gave you the greatest advice ever. This is what idiots do when they say, "Get better at organizing. Okay, next topic." Rather, I want to show you my actual organizational techniques, in hopes that you will be inspired to create an organizational system of your own that works for you.

1 I like Ninjas.

Home

Organization

It's true, organization matters. It is the safety net of success in college. It catches you, repeatedly. You forget when your term paper is due, or you can't find your term paper. You signed up for a different class but forget what it was called. You forget to drop a class. You don't remember your home-work assignments (or where your books are). You forget what day and time your final exam is. The list goes on. And, yes, many of these things only take a second to look up on the Internet, but I wouldn't trust myself to follow through with that either. Organization increases your chances for success – helping you to avoid failure stemming from reasons like the ones listed above. Areas of your life that require organization:

- Your living space
- Your workspace
- How your work space is organized
- Your calendar
- How your schedule is organized

Your living space

To get organized, start with the place where you spend the majority of your time. For most students, this is your room.

My room was always messy. Clothes everywhere, shoes

strewn around the door, trash in and around the trashcan, and random books, papers, and bills on the desk, coffee table, and floor.

A clean room decreases chaos, which, in turn, increases your chances of operating more efficiently. Less clutter in your environment equates to less clutter in your mind. Having a clean room was an enormous help for me.

Start simple.

I bought a good laundry basket my third year of college. It was big enough to hold about two weeks of clothes, it was durable, and it fit in my closet.

I made an effort to put dirty clothes directly into the basket in my closet, and then I would close the closet door. The clothes were now out of sight and mind. After a few days, I didn't have any more clothes on the floor, on my desk chair, or on my bed. My room felt cleaner.

Get a good laundry basket, and put your dirty clothes in it! You only want clothes in your dresser, closet, laundry basket, and on your body.

Your workspace

The next thing you have to tackle is your desk or workspace.

Question: Where is your workspace?

Place an "X" next to your most frequent work area at home.

Bedroom Desk ____
Living Room Coffee Table ____
Dining Room ____
Bed ____

Is your workspace a mess?

Yes ____
No ____

Keeping a tidy workspace is a necessary part of organization. It also relieves tension. Sitting in front of an organized workspace allows a bit of calm to creep in. Things are where they should be. You have the space to work. Your chances of starting work and staying focused while you work increase, because of an uncluttered workspace.

On my desk, I use the "pile system." What is the "pile system?" I am glad you asked. The "pile system" is an organizational technique that I developed where you put things into piles. No, I'm not joking.

Piles are organized by:

- Deadlines - When is the work expected to be complete?
- Importance – How important is the work? Term papers, project outlines, and the like go in this pile.
- Interest – Tedious work, reading assignments, and the least interesting work went in this pile. As due dates loomed, these boring assignments got moved into the deadline pile.

Now, you may be thinking, "That's a stupid idea." And it may be for you, but it works for me.

If I had homework due the next day, the assignment would go on top of the "deadline" pile. It was due the next day, and it would sit there, staring me in the face.

The trick was going through each pile daily. Everything I needed to do was in one of those three piles. Flipping through the piles served as a reminder of what I needed to do today, within the next few days, and within the next few weeks. Coupled with a calendar showing deadlines, I had constant reminders of what work I had to do, and when it was due. Using the pile system, I rarely forgot to do assignments or missed deadlines.

You may prefer using a file cabinet, little shelves or trays for papers, or a different method that you have conjured up.

File cabinets work incredibly well for some people. In my eyes, however, there is too much prep work involved. You need to get a file cabinet, and then get folders and labels, and label all the folders. This seems like a pain. For me, file cabinets are for long-term organization. They're a place you keep financial records and tax information.[2]

Shelves and trays are defined zones to put things, much like my pile system. You are familiar with the "incoming" and "outgoing" trays on someone's desk, I'm sure. If you think the boundaries of a small tray may work for you, then you should get the small tray.

Your calendar

In concert with the pile system, I use a large, monthly, desk-caendar. Until age 23 I had never used a calendar or planner of any kind. I hated them.

Every school I attended gave you a free planner at the beginning of the year. I'd always say to myself, "Oh, this is a great idea." Then a couple of days later I'd throw it away. It got to the point where I loathed planners. If I wrote something down in a planner, say, "Do homework for English tonight," I would be quite pleased with myself. Then, seven hours later, I would open up the planner and read what I had written, and say, "Fuck you planner, don't tell me what to do." I was actually yelling at my own handwriting for telling me what to do with my day. That's how much I hate

2 "Do I claim zero, or one? I can't remember."

planners.

It wasn't so complex in high school when I was constantly around people in the same classes, all day, who were capable of reminding me what was due when. Trying to remember all of my appointments, assignments, meetings, and test dates, without writing anything down became an exhausting task in college. I increasingly forgot what I was supposed to be doing, and where I was supposed to be.[3]

You have to minimize the opportunities to forget things. You must minimize how much mental energy you waste trying to remember dates. Write it down; get it out of your head and onto paper. Stop wasting your time.

The summer before my senior year in college, I bought a large desk calendar and managed to use it. Desk calendars are not magic; your life will not suddenly be organized. It is a great tool when used appropriately, however, in the same way a planner is.

Here is what you do:

Get up, take shower, put on clothes, go to college bookstore. Buy the calendar.

Return home and, if necessary, take calendar out of wrapping. Place calendar on desk.

Log onto Internet and find all syllabi for your classes, including when assignments are due. Print all of them out.

If you do not have a computer or a printer, you must go to the library and print out all of your syllabi there.

Now, the most important step!! You must read through every syllabus and write down when everything is due.[4]

- Write down exam dates. These are the most important.
- Write down due-dates for papers and projects. These

3 I have sat in the wrong classroom for 15 minutes before realizing maybe I'm the one who's in the wrong room, and not all the other students and the professor.

4 I wrote down one month of scheduling at a time. The idea of writing an entire semester seemed daunting, but I felt comfortable with writing down a month's worth.

are as impotant as tests.
- Write down due dates for assignments.
- Write down assigned readings and any other miscellaneous things that you need.
- Double-check your calendar.
- Go outside and challenge a stranger to a rap battle.

Now, when you sit down at your desk to check email or log onto Facebook, you have a reminder, sitting right in front of you, of what is coming up, what is due, and when it is due.

Knowing how large a workload you have from week to week is a great primer for your mind. It readies you to work more efficiently when necessary. When combined with another system of organization (e.g., the "pile system"), you are increasing your exposure to the picture of what work to start on and when to start it.

You may prefer a wall calendar, an agenda, a planner, an email calendar, or your cell phone to a desk calendar.

A guy in my ADHD support group programmed his entire day into his cell phone calendar program. Every hour his cell phone would beep, and he would know exactly what he should be doing that hour. He had his lunch hour mapped out, class times, labs, meetings, homework, study blocks, and free time. Mapping out his day like this enabled him to operate at maximum efficiency. He credited his success in graduate school to using his phone calendar in this way.

Learn how to operate on a medium other than your mind. Whether it be a desk calendar, a planner, a cell phone, or a voice recorder, you must free yourself from the anxiety of trying, and ultimately failing, to remember everything. If you write down the important stuff, you are better suited to focus on the task at hand instead of wasting mental energy trying to remember everything that needs getting done.

No TV in your bedroom

Take the TV out of your bedroom. Get the TV out of there, right now. Your bedroom should be for sleeping, having sex, and, if necessary, working at your desk. Walk over to your TV and put it in the closet or another room. Just get it out of your bedroom.

For years, I believed I needed a TV on to sleep. I realized, however, that I was staying awake until 5:30am staring at the dumbest shows.[5]

The next year, I got rid of the TV. Fine, I didn't get rid of it, but I got it out of my bedroom – it stayed in my closet, unplugged. I thought about plugging it back in. A voice in my head would say, "You know it would be nice to watch TV alone in your room, buddy." This was the voice of the devil! Okay, maybe that's a little intense. It was my inner addict – the part of me that loves the constant stimulation of flipping channels. The TV stayed in the closet, unplugged.

Once my room was free from TV, my life started changing. Coming home after a day of classes, I wouldn't sit in my room for two hours, watching TV. Instead, I would sit down, pull out my notebooks, turn on some music, and look at my desk calendar to see what needed to be done.

Doing anything in your room, anything at all, is better than watching TV.

Without TV your options decrease, which is a good thing. So long as you don't spend hours at a time on Facebook or Internet porn, you can only waste so much time in your room. The likelihood that you pick up a text or do an assignment for class increases in the absence of TV.

It's not that watching TV is inherently bad or wrong.[6] In the battle against yourself, however, TV is the enemy, be-

---

5 Shows like "Text-me TV" and the latest Kevin Trudeau infomercial.

6 TV, in fact, may be inherently bad and wrong.

cause it is so easy to sit there and flip channels. All. Night. Long.

Get the TV out of the room. Trust me.

A couple more things about the place you lay your head

I have learned to appreciate the white noise provided by a fan. Without a fan, my night goes like this:

I am trying to fall asleep, say five minutes have passed, and I am just lying in bed, eyes closed, feeling tired, but not quite asleep. All of a sudden the heat clicks on, and I am aware of this. I hear the furnace at work two floors below me, and then I listen to the sound of the hot air blowing out of the register. The next second, some drunken asshole outside yells something unintelligible. I am aware of this as well. A minute later, I hear keys jingling outside – it turns out that drunken asshole is my roommate. The door opens, and he walks inside. The register clicks off. 25 minutes have now passed, and I'm more awake than when I started.

The fan – or any white noise maker – doesn't block out everything, but it does provide me with something consistent that I can tune-out to while I'm trying to get to sleep. It doesn't change the fact that your furnace is from 1935 and loud as hell, nor that your roommate is a raving alcoholic, but it does turn the volume down on these, somewhat depressing, facts of life.

You need to figure out what type of bed you like. Discover what pillows you like the best. Do you prefer sleeping on a hard, medium or soft mattress? Do you prefer a feather pillow or hotel style? Do you sleep best when the room is cold, but the comforter is warm? Do you sleep best when you have on pajamas? Boxers? A T-shirt? Butt-naked?

Ask yourself these questions. Seek answers as to why on

some nights you sleep well, some not so well, and some not at all. Consider all the factors involved in your being comfortable.

I prefer a hard mattress with a soft mattress pad, one feather pillow, one hard pillow, the room cold, a comforter, boxers, and a fan blowing.

The fan is probably the most important of all these, and I need it. In my youth I discovered that I always slept better during the summer, regardless of how hot it was. I used a fan during the summer. The fan produces white noise, which helps me sleep, so I use the fan year round.

If you need something more serious than a fan to provide you with nighttime ambiance, I can suggest Sleep Sound Audio[7], as well as certain breathing techniques[8]. It may seem weird at first. Having your stereo pumping out "WAAAA-WAAAA-WAAAA" noises all night long isn't exactly normal, but, then again, neither is taking amphetamine every morning. After a few nights, it just might become part of your routine.

Furthermore, keep a pad of paper and a pen next to your bed. You know that feeling when you are lying in bed, and your mind is racing from one thing to another, over and over and over? All you want to do is go to sleep, but you can't. Don't even hesitate. Just grab the pen and put your thoughts down. Anything. Everything.

I don't care if it's important or not, if I write it down on the paper, then I can stop thinking about it. Usually, my mind relaxes after thirty minutes or so. Without the pad and pen, I'll lie there wide-awake for up to three hours.

Let your mind know that all of the things it's thinking about will be remembered and considered tomorrow. Right now you have to go to sleep.

---

7 http://www.quietmindcafe.com/sound-sleep.html

8 There are videos on Youtube of breathing exercises that can help you relax.

The importance of sleep

Being well-rested is one of the best things that you can do for yourself, and, ultimately, college is one of the hardest places to achieve that goal. Then again, I had a hard time with it in middle and high school as well. But I cannot stress this enough: getting the rest you need makes life that much easier.

Apparently, about seven and a half hours is the ideal amount of sleep for adults.[9] Many of us are barely getting six. A well-rested body is able to concentrate longer, function faster, is more resistant to stress and anxiety, and makes you a healthier person. Sleep may also help consolidate information learned during the day, and help you remember what you learned. So, although it's not easy to do, try and get enough rest.

9 There is no magic number for sleep. It varies according to the individual.

School

Class schedules

When I arrived at Michigan State University freshman orientation, we had to choose our class schedules for the upcoming semester. I was paired with a "summer orientation volunteer," and we began scheduling my classes. It may have been because I was hung over, but I somehow didn't notice when she convinced me to take a class that would turn out to be pure hell.

"So, you've got four classes so far" she said, "Do you want to schedule one more?"
"Yeah, why not" I said.
"Okay. We could definitely plug CSE101 in here on Mondays and Wednesdays at 8:00am."
"Wait, what?"
"A lot of times, it's better to get classes like this over with during your first semester, just to get them out of the way."
"I can't take it any later?"
"Well if you did, you would have to move the Interpersonal Communications course to another semester, and you said that you really wanted to take that class, right?"
"Yeah, that's true."
"I mean you can make an eight a.m. class twice a week, trust me." Sounding like a veteran on the subject she followed up with, "Anyways,

the other days of the week your earliest class is 10:20am, so you can sleep in on those days."

"Yeah, you're right" I said. "It shouldn't be a problem twice a week.

Holy shit was I wrong.

The problem here was not that I had a class at eight a.m., or that it was a computer class. I had been going to school at eight a.m. for twelve years, why wouldn't I be able to make this class? I had taken computer classes before, why would this one be different? The problem was the combination of factors: mind numbing, long, and early.

The class itself was absolutely awful. There were two teaching assistants, half-asleep and apathetic, telling us which files to open and important key strokes to know. I wanted to shoot myself in the face. I stopped going to class after a month and a half.

From this experience I learned something that I managed to utilize throughout the rest of my college career: If you do not think you'll go, do not take the class.

You have options when it comes to classes (e.g., what you will take, when you will take it, and location). If you know that you are unable to get to class at 9:00am, then don't take the 9:00am section. Wait until next semester, or take it online during the summer. Whatever you do, take your classes at times that you know you can make.

I had trouble making classes before 9:00am and after 6:00pm. I thought taking classes at 7:00pm would be amazing, a blessing for me. I was wrong. Attending class in the evening was terrible.

After a couple of years of college, I found that I always got the best grades in the classes that began between the hours of 10:00am and 3:00pm. This may seem intuitive to you, but I found it quite the epiphany.

Another thing to consider: what is your ideal length for a

class? I hate sitting still for too long.[10] This was a big problem in high school, and it continued to be an issue in college when I was faced with the prospect of 2 and 3-hour classes. I'm restless, I get bored, and unless the class stimulates my mind in the right ways, I cannot stay engaged longer than 80 minutes, and even then it takes a lot of work to stay focused. This is where ADHD medications may help you the most (we will get to that topic later).

Upon discovering this, I made a point of taking either 50-minute or 80-minute classes. Find out what class length works best for you.

Does it take you 20 minutes to get settled at the beginning of class? If so, 80 minutes may be ideal. After an hour, do you feel like a raccoon in heat trapped inside an aluminum garbage can? If so, stick with the 50-minute classes. Remember, you will not be able to schedule the ideal length class every time, but if you have a choice in the matter, then make the right one.

There is another facet of your course schedule that you need to review: consecutive (back-to-back) vs. non-consecutive classes.

From kindergarten through high school we are, essentially, programmed to go to school early in the morning and then move from class to class for the remainder of the school day. In college we are faced with the option of either spreading our classes out, with some leisure time in-between, or taking classes back-to-back-to-back. I operated better when taking classes back-to-back.

Taking classes spread throughout the day gives you multiple opportunities to blow off class. You wake up late and decide to skip your early class. So, you eat some breakfast and then go to your class at noon. After that, it's 1:20pm and you

10 Sitting here working on this book feels like an exercise in self-flagellation.

don't have class again until 3:00pm. That's enough time to go home and relax for a bit, you say to yourself. When 3:00pm rolls around, however, a buddy of yours suggests that you go play basketball, or smoke a bowl, or watch some stupid TV show, and that sounds much better than going to class. So, out of the three classes that you have that Tuesday, you only made it to one of them.

Having consecutive classes makes it that much easier to attend all of them, because all you need to do is make the first one.

An ideal picture of consecutive classes:

Wake up and go to my first class at 10:20am. First class is 50 minutes and my next one is at 11:40am, but it is a ten-minute walk from building to building. That gives me 20 minutes of down time between classes, which is not enough time for me to go home and do something else. It is just enough time to take a slight detour on my way to class number two and grab a cup of coffee or a sandwich, get to class a few minutes early and work on a crossword. My 11:40am is an 80-minute class, so I'm done at 1:00pm. Instead of scheduling a 3:00pm class here, I'm looking for a start time of 1:20pm for class number three.

Keep the momentum going, because once you are on the move and being productive, there is no need to slow down, relax, and restart. If you go to the first class, then you'll end up going to all of them. There is less room for lethargy, distraction, or apathy to sneak in.

Researching your classes

I had a friend in college who spent hours researching his courses on the school-affiliated website "allmsu.com." Before enrolling, he would spend time looking at teacher ratings, reading student descriptions of the teachers and material, and getting an overall sense of what the class would be like. I always laughed at how much time he spent doing this. And, without fail, I always regretted not doing this when the next semester started. I would have nine books to read in my 'Studies of Asia' class, and he would have three books total. While I spent hours on homework, "B" would tell me, "Today, in class, we spent 45 minutes acting out the life stages of an Emu." What an asshole.

You can discover a lot about the courses you are enrolling in before setting foot in the classroom. However, appropriately interpreting the information you find when reading student reviews is necessary. Try to look at the overall themes of the reviews. Case-by-case you will discover people's grudges, laziness, and unrealistic expectations. Look for the overall answers to these questions:

- Is the lecture engaging?
- Does the professor simply read out of the book?
- What about the professor's teaching style?
    - Do they rely entirely on PowerPoint, or is it lecture and discussion?
- Are the tests multiple choice, short answer, or essays?
- Is there a final?
    - How much is it worth? Is it optional?
- Does the professor take points off for poor attendance?
    - If so, how much can it affect your grade?
- Is there lab work?
    - What percentage of your grade is it?
- Do the majority of students find the class interesting?
- How big is the class?
- Do they have a policy on turning in assignments that is intrinsically idiotic? (e.g., electronic copy must be emailed to T.A. by midnight, and you must turn in a hardcopy by 6:00am the following morning).
- Is the professor a total dick?

You can find out answers to many, if not all of these questions by doing some simple research online. You don't have to be as intense about it as my friend was, but it is an excellent idea to find out as much as possible about any class before signing up.

If people are repeatedly writing that so-and-so is the worst professor ever, see if you can find out why. Do all the comments say that he/she is a dick? A general consensus among strangers may indicate that something is wrong.

Is everybody commenting on specific but different aspects of the course? No overwhelming consensus? It's probably a safe bet that the comments reflect personal preferences and not some glaring defect in the mental make-up of the professor.

Peak brain performance

Our brains have peak hours of operation. Throughout the day, everyone has unique times during which they do things best. Analyze your own experiences, determine how and when you work best, and design your schedule accordingly.

My peak hour of operation was between 10am and 11am in middle and high school. A small window. The first two classes of the day, between 8am – 10am, I caught up on sleep, and then I had about an hour where I could focus. After 11am I was off to the races, and I wouldn't slow down until midnight. I didn't do much homework outside of school, and I didn't create any study habits.

After my first two years in college, I noticed a discernible difference in my grades depending on when the class took place. Noticing this difference occurred over time.

I found I performed best in the classroom between 10am – 12pm and 2pm - 4pm. I could pay attention longer, felt sharper, took better notes, and on test days that's when my mind felt agile.

I wrote papers in the evenings. During the day, my body and mind are too active to sit and write or read for a long time. After a full day, most of my physical energy has been spent, and I'm okay with finally sitting down in front of a computer.

3pm to 7pm was best for short assignments or quick reading. I was more capable of finishing multiple assignments at a fast pace during this time. After 7:00pm, I would generally read or spend my time writing.

After a few years, the picture started to come together. I scheduled classes consecutively, left small gaps in-between for coffee or food, tried to complete homework in the early afternoon, and, in general, wrote papers or read in the evening. Understanding these peak hours of operation led to the beginning of a manageable academic routine.

Study techniques: how you learn best

You need to observe your current study techniques (if you have any) and revise them. This is not an easy task. Ask yourself: how were you trained to study? And is it working for you now?

During the more formative years of our education (I would say between fourth and seventh grade), teachers have a way of telling the class how we should "study for the test." Studying is a big deal during these years (especially closer to fourth grade), because it is still new and not yet ingrained in you – it has yet to manifest itself as the cause of your friend's nervous tic (the half-grin, neck-jerk that you'll always notice), Jeannie's test anxiety ("I think I'm ready, I mean, I studied all week. I dunno, I hope I'm ready, I really need to do good on it…"), and feelings of hopelessness (I'm going to fail), depression (I'm worthless), regret (I shouldn't even have taken this fucking class), and, of course, the fleeting feeling of success. But I digress.

Study techniques are only briefly mentioned during these early years. You never spend an entire class period or semester learning how to study. It's assumed that if you have a book and some notes, and you stare at them long enough, or make flashcards,[11] that you will be ready for the test. And when you don't do well on the test, teachers/parents assume it is because you simply, "Didn't spend enough time studying."

Study techniques are slow to evolve – we are taught study techniques by our teachers (and the occasional bark of a parent about what "I used to do…"), who have been taught how to study by both teachers and parents, who have been taught how to study by their teachers and parents, who have been taught by… well, you get the idea.

You were given the illusion of having formed your own ways to study – at the young age when study techniques start to take shape it is nearly impossible to parry away adult guidance. You were taught how to study by people whose basic wiring differs from your own.[12] For most, this is just fine, because their operating systems are closely related. However, if your parents don't have ADHD, and your teacher doesn't have ADHD, and the people they learned study techniques from didn't have ADHD (etc…) then how could they possibly know the best way for you to study? You need to find out what works best for you.

For years I relied strictly on study guides – the list of "topics" that may or may not be included on an exam which professors hand out or email a week before the test. My study techniques were poorly thought out, and they weren't tailored to my strengths.

A day before the exam, two days if I was on top of my game, I would print/pull out the study guide. I'd write down

11 (Insert any "traditional" method here)

12 Would an alien have success teaching Japanese to a tree?

each topic listed on the guide on a separate, white piece of unlined paper, and then spend the next six to twelve hours going through notes, books, PowerPoint slides, and lectures defining and describing these topics in full detail. Once finished writing everything down, it was 4am, and I was in possession of 10 to 20 white, information-packed pieces of paper. The next five hours were spent "memorizing" these pages, after which I'd show up to the exam with bloodshot eyes, smelling like stale smoke and coffee, wondering if the exam's, "going to go well?" Sometimes there were friends who joined in on this odd, sleep depriving, anxiety-inducing ritual, but most times I was alone in my misery.[13]

This study technique failed me, because:

- I never had enough time to study – I never started early enough.
- I wasn't engaged by this technique (i.e., the act of transcribing for hours and hours allowed me to be a passive participant, never gaining my full attention).
- Once I had written everything down, I tried using rote memorization (a technique which has literally never worked for me).
- I was exhausted when it was time to take the test, and I couldn't be counted on to pay attention to, I don't know, anything more involved than walking.

I had been studying this way since middle school, and it was inefficient and tedious.[14] Finally, I stopped wasting my time with study guides. So, what changes did I make?

I started asking myself questions while studying (e.g., was

13 This is a literal description of studying during my first three years of college.

14 This method may work just fine for some, especially when studying starts earlier than one or two days before the exam. And, I have to say, I usually scored above 75% using this method, but I also got a number of scores below 65% - in no way excelling, but rather maintaining my own status quo.

that an important point? How does this paragraph relate to the previous section? How much of the past two pages relate to what was lectured on? Would these definitions and examples make for good test questions? And how? Etc.). Then I took the time to formulate both long and short answers.

These answers ranged from one-word responses to constructing fully formed arguments on a topic – arguments such as these could be summarized in four or five bullet-points or by scribbling a keyword in the margin that would bring back a train-of-thought. In the same way that acronyms or mnemonics aid your memory for a list (e.g., Kings Play Chess On Fat Girls' Stomachs), asking myself questions while I was reading the material for the first, or third, time, created different links and pathways as a reader, test-taker, and test-maker (or, at least, question-asker) that I hadn't been making before.

I created more connections between the material and my mind on multiple levels, which enabled me to recall facts, theories, and arguments with a speed and accuracy I had been missing.

I asked questions in different ways depending on the material. If a test relied heavily on a textbook, I'd write questions in the margins while reading. If there were questions within the text (e.g., review questions) I'd underline them and scribble the main points of the question in the margin – gaining an understanding of what concepts were important to the book's author. Reviewing material became a more natural process, because I would flip through the few chapters, look at what I'd underlined and written in the margins, and regain a picture of what the chapter was about and what important questions and concepts the chapters centered on.[15]

This process was quick (meaning it could be done more

15 This new study technique relied much more on my reading the material, a battle in-and-of-itself. But it was a different type of reading, a more active or mentally involved reading.

than once, unlike the study guide transcription) and it kept me engaged in the activity (jumping around from page-to-page is more akin to how I naturally read). Reading my own notes and scribbles in the margins of the text brought back memories of what I had read. It provided a more efficient way to review than any amount of rewriting and rote memorization could. I started seeking a deeper understanding of the material, instead of attempting to memorize a study guide. This technique became the most reliable way for me to understand and remember the material from a textbook.[16]

If the test included material from PowerPoint slides as well, I would approach studying in a slightly different manner. But, I will explain that in a minute. First, a word about PowerPoint.

Associations with Personality

- **Openness** most closely related to:
  - Reflective/Complex music (Blues, Jazz, Classical, Folk)
  - Also intense/rebellious music (Rock, Alternative, Heavy Metal), but weaker relationship
- **Extraversion and Agreeableness**:
  - Upbeat/Conventional (country, soundtracks, religious, pop)
  - Energetic/Rhythmic (rap/hip-hop, soul/funk, electronica/dance)
  - Extraversion somewhat correlated with Intense/rebellious (Rock, Alternative, Heavy Metal)
- **Conscientiousness**
  - Small association with Upbeat/Conventional
- **Emotional stability** not associated with any preference

I fucking hate PowerPoint.[17] Unfortunately, too many pro-

16 This is dependent on the type of test you are facing. Sometimes, no matter how much you hate it, you have to simply memorize definitions or dates or reactions, and no amount of deeper understanding will help you (at times like these, I can count on scoring 15% lower on a test).

17 See shitty PowerPoint slide above.

fessors rely on it – at least, they did at MSU. For me, there was nothing worse than sitting in class with a professor who would write an entire sermon on 30 PowerPoint slides and then read them verbatim.

In my eyes, this is not teaching.

PowerPoint should only be used as a visual guide to a mainly oral presentation. If you see a good PowerPoint presentation, it may blow your mind. They are that rare. A good example can be found at:

http://www.ted.com/talks/larry_lessig_says_the_law_is_strangling_creativity.html

The slides are not cramped with text, and the speaker does not rely on them in any fashion. They facilitate the lecture by providing the speaker with a simple, visual aspect to his presentation.

When a professor puts up three giant paragraphs onto a slide and then, at the top of it, has a stupid little animation of a guy looking through a microscope or a magician, for example, I start staring at the useless animation, ignoring what the professor is saying, stop taking notes, and hating the idiot that put it there.

18 "It's Magic, and I'm an asshole!"

You may have to alter your study techniques for a test that relies heavily on PowerPoint.

If you have the option of printing out the slides before class, you must do it.[19] Pick out the slides that are, "important" and concentrate on that information. PowerPoint presentations usually include many definitions. Pay attention to these. Then, try to find out what material from the textbook was included in the PowerPoint slides. Make a note of any material that is only on the slides, and ask yourself the following:

Is this information important?

Did this information get any special treatment in class?

If you have already done the assigned reading and have been to the lectures, then you can trust your gut on whether or not the PowerPoint slides are important. I used the PowerPoint pages in the same way as the textbook – I'd write in the margins, make notes, ask myself questions and attempt to gain a deeper understanding of what we'd be tested on. This was the key to altering my study techniques.

I make connections and can think logically once I have grasped the overall aspects of a subject. I can work my way through multiple choice, short answer, and essay questions with relative ease so long as I have wrapped my head around the basics of a subject or concept. I did not understand this about myself until I changed my study techniques – until I changed my approach to learning.

Forget how you have been taught to learn (or study), and teach yourself. ASK YOURSELF:

- How do I retain information?
- Visual/Verbal
    - Good with notes on the board in class and learning from textbook readings.

19 I always had trouble doing this.

- Visual/Nonverbal
    - Benefit from videos, diagrams, and flowcharts.
- Tactile/Kinesthetic
    - Like hands-on activities, building things, physically manipulating your learning materials.
- Auditory/Verbal
    - Prefer discussion and lecture; like to have a conversation about the material with other people.
- When preparing for a test, do I always wish for more time to study?
    - Is the problem related to the efficiency of my study techniques or time management leading up to the test?
- What study environment is best for me?
    - Complete silence?
    - With music playing in the background?
    - With another person or a group?
    - What timeframe allows me to study best?
    - Do I study best in short bursts?
    - 20 minutes at a time, with five-minute breaks in-between?
    - Does it take a long time to start studying, but once at it I can sustain my attention over a long period of time?
        - If so, avoid breaks.
- Do I like reading off of a computer?
- Do I respond well to visual stimuli?
    - Flowcharts?
    - Diagrams?
    - Flashcards?
- Do I retain information well after explaining my position to someone?
- Reading out-loud?

Answering these questions will enable you to start adjusting and refining your own techniques to study more efficiently.

Study routines and habits

If you've ever seen a boxing match, you always see the fighters in the dressing rooms warming up before the fight. They go through their combinations, hit the mitts, and do some shadowboxing. This routine activates their mind and body, preparing them for the battle to come. If a fighter steps into the ring without a sweat going and isn't warmed up properly, he will surely get out to a slower start than his opponent. It's the same with studying. You need to warm up the brain prior to the battle with the books.

Routines guide me toward a task, and, therefore, divert me from distraction. When creating a study routine, keep in mind the image of the boxer warming up – it just takes a few minutes to get ready, but the payoff is big.

Creating a study routine

Include anything you want in your study routine. Seriously, anything, as long as it doesn't include TV. If the routine is consistent, it should work. All your routine must do is wake your brain up, get those gears moving, and then make it painfully obvious that the next thing you are going to do is study. That is it. The main aspects of a routine are:

- Finding your study spots: the places where you work best.
- Doing the warm-up: what you do to get your brain

moving.
- Execute: knowing what your plan of attack is for that session, and when it's time to start studying.

When I lived in the dorms the first two years of college, I rarely studied at my desk. There were too many possible distractions. During this time, I frequented the library. I studied at two particular tables in the library. When I sat down at these tables, my mind knew what it was there to do. This is the main idea behind the study spot; it is a familiar place that triggers your mind into study mode.

Doing the warm-up involves anything that, in a short amount of time, gets you ready to work. My warm-up was simple. Upon arriving at either the library or coffee shop, I would grab a drink, and sit down at my table. I'd take out my books and notebooks, and place them around me. This made the transition to studying easy. When it was time to work I could simply begin. Then I would start on that day's crossword puzzle, and I'd work on it until I felt I couldn't get any more answers. When I reached that point, I'd start studying – the execution.

As you can see, this routine was simple. I'd go to a place that I was used to (an environment conducive to studying), I'd grab a drink (letting my brain know that we would not go thirsty throughout this traumatic experience), I'd set up my workspace (preparing the tools necessary to study), I'd do a crossword (to get my mind warmed up), and when I couldn't get any further on the crossword[20] I'd open a textbook or my notes. This routine readied my mind to get work done.

You may do things differently. Maybe you prefer the basement of your house, where there is only one light bulb and

20 This was my 'timer' of sorts. You may need to set an actual timer. Some days I would spend five minutes on the crossword, and some days I would spend 45 minutes on it. This was easier for me to stomach than placing a strict time limit on my warm-up.

complete silence. Maybe you like doing a Sudoku instead of a crossword, or reading the news gets your brain moving best. Whatever you prefer is fine. Find something that prepares you for the task at hand - a cascade of events that once started is followed through to completion. When you find and implement your routine, it will become much easier to start studying.

Throwing stars

It should come as a surprise to many of us that the throwing star has been phased out as a respectable weapon. The star (Shuriken, in Japanese) is small, lightweight, and deadly – giving it the holy trinity of street-wise weaponry. And yet, for some inexplicable reason, it has suffered a massive dip in popularity over the past 150-200 years. Surely, this is inversely correlated to the ever-evolving, ever-popular handgun. In my eyes, the handgun provides a fraction of the awesomeness that throwing stars do.

When comparing handguns and throwing stars, it is important to remember that you rarely need to kill/maim an individual who is further than 20 feet away from you. In lieu of this, a throwing star provides, quite simply, the same amount of range as a handgun. Furthermore, a throwing star is silent, even more silent than a handgun with a silencer on its barrel. The only sounds you hear when you throw a throwing star are, "Ahhhhhhh," and, "Was that a fucking throwing star?" Yes, it was, now have another to the face.

Throwing stars can also be kept on your person in a myriad of ways – in a pocket, up your sleeve, or taped to your leg. Now, granted, handguns can be kept in these places too, but if you have a gun in your pocket you don't also put your keys in that pocket. With a throwing star, in pocket, you have the option of putting keys in there as well. Huge plus.

Like handguns, throwing stars come in all different shapes and sizes, so if you're questioning whether there's enough variety for your individual taste or personality-type, fear not, there is.

Last but not least, throwing stars are used by ninjas. Meaning once you log one kill/maim with a throwing star you become a ninja. This is a known fact in Japan. No belt color, no bullshit. "What's my belt color? I kill/maim people with throwing stars, that's my belt color, friend." When you use a handgun you don't automatically become a sniper, do you? No, you don't. It takes years of training and dedication to become a sniper. But when you use a throwing star in the way it was meant to be, you are a ninja. That's all there is to it.

So, the next time you are considering what weapon you need to deliver justice with, simply ask yourself, "Do I want to be a ninja?" The decision should make itself.

Picking courses: what do you like learning about?

Coming out of high school, I was certain that I wanted to own a bar. I remember thinking, "Owning a bar would be awesome." So I talked to a few people and they told me, in an oddly Confucian manner, that one who aspires to own a bar should study "Hospitality Business." And that is exactly what I did.

I started off with Hospitality Business, but after one class decided it wasn't for me – I could have given the subject more of a chance, I suppose, but I just knew I wasn't into it. I found the class particularly boring. I convinced myself I didn't need to waste time and money on courses that tell you that the best way to get someone to come to your business is by consistently giving them a reach-around the instant they park their car in your business's lot.[21] Seems like a pretty intuitive business model.

So, after trashing the "bar-owner" dreams, I became "undecided" for a year-and-a-half. This new title was better suited to handle the burden that was my incapacity to make decisions. I felt comfortable with it. Deciding by not making a decision, not taking a stand. After my second year in college, I took a year off. Regrouped. Worked.

When it was time to re-enroll, I chose Pre-Nursing.[22] And I put in a lot of effort. But, after completing all of those arduous science courses and getting rejected after a half-hearted application to nursing school, I switched once more, in my fifth year, and finally received a degree in psychology. Maybe I should have stuck with my gut feelings about what I wanted to study, but part of me thinks that I became a more versatile student, because I took such a wide variety of courses.

These skids and false starts taught me this: take courses that interest you and that you excel at. If you enjoy the courses, make it your focus and get the degree.

I struggled to understand that it only, kind-of matters what you study in undergrad. There are many different paths that lead from one area of study to another.[23] It is just as important to spend time on critical thinking skills, at internships, or pursuing letters of reference. You are better served if you learn about some shit[24] that captivates you. If you enjoy a subject, like learning about it, find the readings interesting, and think the material is challenging and stimulating, then you are more likely to excel. Forget everybody who tells you to study this or focus on that. How can they know what is right for you?

---

21 Yes, this is pretty much all I have taken away from my Intro to Hospitality Business course.

22 At this time, 2005-2006, it was as if every newspaper article wrote about how easy it was to get a job as a nurse.

23 I know an English major that owns a restaurant, a Psychology major in medical school, and Zoology major who ended up in law school.

24 "What did you learn today?" "Oh, you know, some shit."

Political Science, Literature, Philosophy and Psychology: the four subjects that I could have majored in. I performed well in each of these subjects. Attending class was easy, because I enjoyed the material, lectures, and discussions. My brain was wired for these courses. Abstract thinking, creating and backing up ideas, and writing research papers were all things that I excelled in. Even so, it took a few years for me to realize this. Psychology was the best mixture for my natural skills. It involved theoretical and abstract thinking. It has a strong and burgeoning basis in research. I found the readings interesting. I enjoyed the lectures and discussions. So, after a few years for me to figure out what I'd get my degree in, the choice finally smacked me in the face. I was good at it, and I liked it. Once you realize this is what matters, the decision of what to major in takes care of itself.

Struggling with the decision of what to study? Here are some questions to guide your thinking:

- What do you most enjoy doing?
    - Reading
    - Writing
    - Drawing
    - Discussion/Debate
    - Research
    - Math
    - Foreign languages
    - Working outside
    - Working with your hands
    - Working with people
    - Helping people
    - None of the above
- What classes have you truly enjoyed in the past?
    - Did you enjoy reading the textbooks in these classes?
        - Did you even read the textbooks?

    - Did you even buy the textbooks?
- Are you better at multiple-choice tests or essay-based tests?
- What is your favorite section to read in a newspaper?
- What is your greatest skill?
- What are your hobbies?
- How much does money motivate you?

When contemplating what courses to take and what to study remember why you are in school in the first place.

Learn about things that interest you and subjects that you are passionate about. Sometimes it's right in front of your face. All you have to do is realize it.

Professors: the good and the bad

I have had good – even great – professors, but I have also had a few morons. At a large university, the professor accounts for only a percentage of the class. Every class can be broken down into smaller parts.

- How does the professor teach?
    - Engaging teaching style
    - Discussion
    - Boring teaching style
    - Reads out of book
- What is the format of the class?
    - Tests are
        - Multiple choice
        - Essay or short answer
    - Any group projects?
    - Term papers

        - What percentage of grade?
- What you expect from yourself
    - Grade-wise?
        - 4.0
        - 3.5
        - 3.0
        - 2.5
    - Time commitment?
        - 1 hour per day
        - 30 minutes per day
        - 1 hour per week
        - 30 minutes per week
- What you are required to do for the class
    - Show up to class
    - Do the work assigned
    - Spend time in laboratories
- The work you actually do for the class
    - All
    - None
    - Somewhere in the middle
- What the professor expects from you
    - It's a fair question. What does he or she expect out of you?
        - Perfection
        - Mediocrity
        - Failure

This can be a pie chart!! Everybody likes Pie Charts![25]

Characteristics of the professor matter, but s/he is only a part of the whole. Sure, s/he controls the grades, the format of the class, and has expectations of you. But everything else

25 There was going to be a pie chart, but I couldn't figure out how to create one in my old version of Microsoft Word. So, instead, I got frustrated and abandoned the idea.

is dependent on what you bring to the table.

My favorite professors shared certain qualities:

- They were organized.
- There was simplicity in the structure of the course.
- Lectures were engaging.
- They had a system in place for tests, assignments, and papers, and they stuck to it.
- They encouraged discussions.
- They were open to questions.
- They didn't rely on PowerPoint.
- They kept office hours or some sort of availability.
- They didn't stray too far from relevant material.
- They understood that students have other things going on in their lives, besides the class.

The professors that I hated also shared certain qualities:

- They read straight from the book and considered it a lecture.
    - Which, in turn, made you want to slam a fork into your eye.
- They were condescending.
- They were consistently disorganized.
- They were too reliant on teaching assistants.
- They used every type of electronic system for homework, group projects, calendars, etc. without regard as to whether or not it made sense or was, indeed, a more efficient or useful system.

Regardless of the personality traits and teaching styles of your professors, you still have to read the texts, do the assignments, write the papers, take notes, and study. Matching up well with a particular teaching style will make the class more enjoyable, and it may improve your performance, but it is not the only determinant of your end grade (as is evidenced by the pie chart).

To find professors that match your learning style, you need to understand your own learning style. Once you figure that out, expand your vision. Find out which professors are best by asking friends or other students in class. Look online, or drop in on classes to get an idea of whom you're dealing with.

Generally speaking, each academic department has its own kind of teaching style. Philosophy courses are usually lecture and discussion based. Large introductory psychology courses will use a lot of PowerPoint and pull most of their material from a single textbook. Math and chemistry departments may still use chalkboards for some reason. The individual professors may be different, but within departments, teaching styles tend to conform. Match up your learning style to a professor's teaching style, find a subject you enjoy, and success will come much more easily than if you're still trying to learn via an outdated form of osmosis. You are putting yourself in a position to succeed by knowing your learning style, what subjects you like, and how the professor teaches.

Finding and using resources

No matter how much you plan ahead, or how prepared you are, sometimes you need help. That's the way life is. Profound, I know. In no particular order, here are some resources that helped me:

- The Resource Center for People with Learning Disabilities (RCPD) at Michigan State University
- Speaking with counselors
    - People who have a general interest in your well-being, can provide a different perspective, and listen to problems or issues in your life.

- Speaking with academic advisors
    - Answer questions regarding scheduling, course loads, and different degrees or careers.
- Attending professors' office hours
- Attending teaching assistants' office hours
    - Provide you with direction on homework, papers, or tests. Review rough drafts.
- Extended time on tests
- Tutors
    - Will spend time working with you on the most specific of problems that you have trouble understanding, for the right price. Helpful and patient people.
- Study groups
    - Useful way to engage yourself in studying. Discussion is helpful. Also, gives you the opportunity to compare notes and discover what areas of class other people are focusing on.
- Study partner
    - Similar to study group, but you can usually get a little more focused back-and-forth with just one other person.
- Any type of "center" that your school has that can provide help
    - Math center
        - Help with math homework
    - Writing center
        - Help with term papers
    - General resource centers, etc.
        - Help with other subjects

Have you considered getting a tutor before, but then convinced yourself you didn't need one? Have you wanted to go talk with a professor during office hours but then decided to blow it off? Maybe it's time you follow through.

Help can be good and there is no shame in seeking it. The most important resources I used were: Professors' office hours and the Resource Center for people with Learning Disabilities.

Resource one: talking to professors

Talk to your professors, ask questions, and voice concerns during office hours or after class. It is an opportunity to put in face time and to work through any questions, one-on-one. This is also your chance to narrow down what will be on a test or what the professor is specifically looking for on a term paper.

For the most part, professors are decent people. If you seek their help, they will provide you with something. It may not be exactly what you are looking for, but it will be something. In my mind, sitting down and talking with the professor is your best resource available.

I once had a biology exam, comprised of about 80 questions. Because I received extra time on my tests, I had an hour and twenty minutes to finish the exam, compared to the usual 50 minutes. I was in a room by myself, with a white-noise maker – what I would call "optimal testing conditions." Everything was going fine for the first two or three questions. I remember this scenario vividly, because I could not believe what happened next. The fourth question on the test was about a microorganism that thrives best in temperatures far below zero – and the question used the word "Arctic." That was it. Simple enough.

But, for some asinine reason, when I saw the word "Arctic," I started thinking about penguins. "Do penguins live in the North or South pole?" I wondered. I didn't have the answer, but I knew for damned sure that some penguins inhabited the Galapagos Islands – warm water penguins, which, clearly, differed from their cold-dwelling counterparts. I wondered what Darwin thought when he saw penguins in the warm waters of the Galapagos. He must have said to himself, "What the fuck is that penguin doing in such warm water?" Then I thought, "Did Darwin even study penguins?" Wasn't he all about finches? I remember this one time when I was six my mom put out a bird feeder in the winter and got finches to come to it. Wait, were they finches or sparrows?

This was what I call the "mental carnival,"[26] and it spanned about 35 minutes. Because it was a tough Biology exam, I was rereading each question three to five times, trying to stay diligent. But I was off task, and when time was up I had finished only 50 of the 80 questions. I was dumbfounded. I had spent half of my test time thinking about penguins and other birds. Insert fork into eyeball.

I asked my RCPD counselor what I should do, and she told me to hurry over to the biology building and ask the professor if I could finish the test. Luckily, prior to this incidence of massive failure, I had spoken with the professor a few times, and when I explained that I had gotten off task and wasn't able to finish the test, he told me to pull a desk into his office, and hand it to his secretary when I was finished.

Had I not spoken to him throughout the semester, the professor may have rejected my request to finish the test. Take the time to talk with your professors, because if you are in a bind, they'll be more apt to help you out. The alternative is being just another face in the crowd, and you won't reap too many benefits from that.

Resource two: the RCPD

The Resource Center for People with Learning Disabilities (RCPD, for short) helped me with many things throughout my career at MSU. The RCPD gave me access to tutoring, extended-time on and optimal conditions for tests, a support

---

26 That day's main attractions at the mental carnival were penguins, Charles Darwin, and finches, with a sideshow of failure.

group, and a counselor. If you have access to a place like this, I would highly suggest using it.

From my first semester on, the RCPD assigned me a counselor, Mrs. H., who gave me advice, steered me in certain directions when I needed steering, and maintained a general interest in my well-being throughout my years at MSU. Mrs. H. also organized the ADHD Support Group, where students got together and asked questions, discussed problems and solutions, and anything else about life that was on their plate at the time. This also was a very useful resource. We discussed which medicines worked well for different individuals, what study technique or organizational technique someone had discovered, good tutors, any drastic issues people were dealing with, and their great accomplishments. In fact, my experience with this group is what gave me the idea to write this book.

Resource three: extended time on tests

I was granted extended time on my tests in high school, and I was allowed to continue receiving extended time through the RCPD when I arrived at college.

I am already a slow reader, and I'm especially slow when it comes to more technical reading. As the test questions got harder over the years, the extended time became a blessing in certain areas and a curse in others.

When it came to technical classes like pathophysiology, biology, microbiology, and neurobiology, I used the extended time, because the majority of questions on these tests are packed with information. Longer questions and tougher scientific jargon would force me to reread each question a few times to make sure I understood it correctly. For these types of courses, the extra time was a blessing. I needed the time to slow down, read every word, and catch all the details. Without extra time I would've been screwed.

After a couple of years, however, I noticed there were

classes with tests that I didn't need the extended time on. Philosophy, English, Political Science, and some Psychology courses had short questions (i.e., one sentence leading to a multiple choice question), or open-ended ones (i.e., a few sentences leading to a short answer or essay). For these classes, I found that it was better to let my mind go as fast as it wanted. If I had essays or short-answers to write, I would let loose. If they were simple definition questions, matching, or multiple-choice (not my strong suit) where the questions weren't too technical, I would try to execute faster so that I wouldn't dwell on any one question or second-guess myself out of a correct answer. Using this strategy, my test performance improved.

Find your available resources and use them. If Biology is going horribly, then you should speak with the professor or get a tutor. If you aren't finishing your tests, see what options you have for getting extra time. Office hours. Study groups. Whatever. As you read the list of resources, if you've thought of seeking help in one of those areas before, do it. Don't mull it over, just go and see what it's like. It could be exactly what you need.

Life

Ramen noodles

Let me write, for a minute, about my unconditional love for ramen noodles. I'm talking about the small packs of flash-fried noodles that cost twenty-five cents a pop, or five for a dollar from your local grocery store. Yes, those ones.

When I was roughly three years old, my Korean babysitter introduced me to ramen noodles. She might as well have introduced me to heroin, as far as I'm concerned. During her tenure, we frequently ate ramen in its traditional form, as soup. I was in love.

By the age of six I was allowed to cook ramen noodles by myself, and I discovered the greatest thing about them – straining the water from the noodles before adding the flavor packet made for an immeasurably greater experience. It was the only time I was allowed to use the stove. Boil water, add noodles, cook for three minutes, strain water, stir in flavor packet, and then have your taste buds touched by Jesus Christ. My parents trusted me with this procedure, barely.

I ate ramen almost every day, for lunch, one summer.

After a few years of perfecting the mechanics of my new technique, I began to experiment with the addition of black and white pepper, crushed red pepper, and chili powder. I had perfected my technique by age fourteen.

My love for ramen noodles is undying. I still eat them twice a week. They are still delicious. They are still cheap. They still take less than five minutes to prepare. I am still in love.

Keeping busy: don't slow down, speed up

Have you heard the theory that ADHD is actually an evolutionary adaptation?

It seems that back in the day, the cavemen who didn't have "ADHD" were so oblivious to their surroundings they would get eaten by crazy-awesome saber-tooth tigers. So, over years and years, cavemen eventually became a little more vigilant. Instead of being oblivious to environmental stimuli, caveman 2.0 was somewhat aware of his surroundings. However, he was still eaten by some other crazy prehistoric animal.

Then caveman 3.0 was released. He was hyper-vigilant. Everyone was always telling him to shut up, "Ugh," they'd say, "Uga guh guh guha." He was always climbing trees and then falling out of them, and when it was time to paint on the walls, he was pacing around the cave telling everybody else that wall-painting was fucking boring to watch. Caveman 3.0 was also the best hunter and didn't get eaten by crazy animals as often, because he was more aware of his surroundings than the previous versions of cavemen. He was the ancestor of you and I.

I like this idea. Some people think ADHD is a societal diagnosis, others think it stems from slower development of the frontal lobe, and some people think it's caused by exposure to lead or pesticides. I like to think that we are better models of an always-adapting entity. We think faster, we have more energy, we take more risks (for better and worse), and we can adapt quicker. From this angle, who wouldn't want ADHD?

Think about computers. Would you want to own the shitty Macintosh from 1988, or do you want the amazing new laptop that runs faster, longer, and does so much more? I say we are the faster operating system of the human race, and society has simply refused to change for us.

The education system says that we should slow down because we are too active[27] in the classroom, so we get prescribed drugs. Shouldn't we be looking for ways to change the school system that was created in the 1700s, a time when most people were retarded by today's standards?[28] Well, who knows how long until we see any societal change on this issue, so in the meantime, I say, don't slow down, speed up.

Take a second to think about your ideal day. Would you be sitting on the couch all day watching TV? Would you spend the entire day sitting in a classroom? Or, would your day be packed with places to be and things to do? Work, school, friends, sports, food, relationships, and adventure[29] can be packed into every day if you speed up.

Instead of fighting it, try to embrace your energy. When other people are slowing down or getting tired, we are still operating at mach-five. My productivity increases when my days are packed. I am always happier when I have more to do. People wondered how I managed to take 12 credits, work 35 hours a week, and train as an amateur boxer. Simple, I am happiest when I stay busy.

Filling your days with things to do and places to be enables you to do two important things: Expend energy and enjoy accomplishments.

You want to use your energy. You want to get it out of your body. Don't sit around feeling antsy, looking for things to do but never doing anything. Get it out of your system and do as much as possible.

Speeding up, embracing your energy, and packing your days with things to do also increases your chances of getting things done. Allow yourself better odds. That's all.

It's not a hard concept to understand, but it is an important one. Enjoying accomplishments is what it's all about, so

27 This is often called, "Being disruptive."

28 I hear some charter schools are attempting new ways of engaging kids in the classroom. All hope may not yet be lost.

29 It is often hard to add adventure to an already full schedule, but I like trying.

give yourself the opportunity to succeed as many times as possible throughout each day.

Finding a routine: embracing habits

Do you have an addictive personality? I know I do. As a kid I was addicted to apple juice. I drank more apple juice than was healthy for any four year-old to consume. The doctor instructed my mom to deny me any apple juice – at the time this was devastating. Not too long after, I became addicted to pickles, and I would eat them until my stomach hurt. I think I remember getting a green rash once, but this could just be a half-remembered embellishment. After the pickles, came Bubblicious chewing gum. I would stuff an entire pack in my mouth at once, and chew and chew and chew until my jaw was sore from the leathery mass.

Over the years came the "love-affairs" with weed, cigarettes, coffee…[30] you get the idea. My addictive personality, I believe, makes me more susceptible to habit-forming behavior – and it makes no difference as to whether these are positive or negative habits.

A key to success in managing the positives and negatives of habitual behavior: the number of good habits must outweigh the number of bad habits.[31]

To start a new habit, it takes anywhere from two weeks to two months of doing that new thing every day.[32] If you start running, cooking yourself breakfast, playing guitar before bed, or doing some homework[33] every day, at the end of a month, this new thing will probably be a habit. If you con-

---

30 …And green apples, biting my nails, fruit snacks, gummy bears, Mad Magazine, bmxing, skateboarding, and boxing.

31 If the bad habit is a serious drug addiction, then this formula probably will not apply.

32 Time is dependent on difficulty (i.e., Drinking a glass of water every morning versus running five miles every morning).

33 Yes, there are bad habits that could potentially be listed here, but I'm staying positive.

tinuously add new good habits to your daily routine, then over time you will be living a vastly different lifestyle. To do this properly you must embrace your habits and find a routine.

I'm not asking you to sacrifice spontaneity in life and succumb to monotony, but I am asking you to take a look at your current routines and habits.

Having a healthy breakfast every day is a good thing, so why not make this a habit? Wake up, take a shower, and eat breakfast. Do this every day for a month. Habit formed.

Studying in-between your first and second classes – if you have enough time – is a good thing. Make it a habit? Why not? When your first class is over go to the library and study for an hour. Every time you have this class. Repeat for two weeks. New habit.

Have a lot of mental energy left after a few classes? Well, when you get out of your last class for the day, eat a snack and then do some reading. Read every day for 30 minutes after your last class. Three weeks. You get the idea.

Habits I formed during college:

- Coffee and breakfast in the morning.
- Boxing gym or some type of intense workout for two hours a day, three to five days a week.
- Studying for thirty minutes or more in-between classes.
- A minimum of thirty minutes of assigned reading in the early evening.

I am throwing these examples at you, because I am unaware of what specific areas in your life or academic career are lacking. But that doesn't mean there aren't some. It should be painfully obvious to you, and if it's not ask a friend. They'll remind you of the things you are consistently bitching about, or things that you could improve on. Find time in your day and do something new. Once. Then twice. Continue doing it, even if you don't want to. Keep doing it. After a few weeks it will be part of your life, and you won't even remember, or believe, what life was like without your new habit or routine.

Whether or not you will be successful all depends on your motivations for wanting to create a new habit, your discipline in starting and continuing a new habit, and whether or not you're actually ready for this new habit in the first place.

A buddy of mine says, at its simplest level, forming or creating a new habit comes down to discipline. He talks about running every morning. After a few days, when your muscles are sore, the last thing you want to do is go run. He argues that maintaining this change comes down to the discipline you have to continue with the new act, regardless of what you want to do (i.e., the discipline to wake up and run, even though you want to sleep in).

I believe he is correct. However, I also think a large part of it boils down to what is motivating you, specifically, intrinsic versus extrinsic motivation.[34] If your reasons for change come from within, then your ability to implement that change becomes greater. You want change and are ready for something to happen, and that readiness makes creating a new set of habits more likely.

Being extrinsically motivated may work for the duration of the external stimuli – whether that external stimuli is a test, a class, a semester, the need to please your parents, etc. But once that stimulus has ended, the chances of keeping that habit going are diminished. Therefore discipline, in my eyes, is a necessary component of creating change, but the motivation behind it provides longevity to maintaining that

34 Intrinsic motivation refers to motivation that is driven by an interest or enjoyment in the task itself, and exists within the individual rather than relying on any external pressure. Extrinsic motivation comes from outside of the individual (yay psychology 101). Playing socccer because you love soccer versus volunteering because you need 100 hours of community service to avoid jail.

change.

Timing is another important aspect of making a change. By timing I mean, where you are in your life. Are you actually ready for this change? Does your environment support you trying to make this change? When attempting to create new habits or get rid of old ones, you will find resistance from internal and external sources, and it helps to know whether you are actually ready for a change.

Embracing the right habits is an essential part of mitigating some of the negative aspects of ADHD, allowing you to be more successful in your pursuits, whatever they are. If you think that you can create and maintain a habit that could have a large positive impact on your academic career or personal life, then examine what new habits could be added to your routine and add them.

Athletics: the advantage of excercise

When I was 20, I started competing as an amateur boxer. The workouts were grueling. Monday through Friday from 5:00pm to 7:00pm at the gym I would jump rope, run, hit the heavy-bag, double-end bag, speed bag, hit the mitts with coach, and spar. Exhausted at the end of a workout, I'd go home, make dinner, and pass out around 9:30pm. It was summer, and I was working for a rental company from 7:00am to 5:00pm. The job involved lifting tables and chairs, setting up giant party tents, and sledging stakes into the ground. My entire day was pretty much one big workout.

At the end of each day I was exhausted, and I was sleeping better than ever before. My energy store was depleted during the day and replenished come morning. This was a good thing, and I've tried to continue this routine. It was in my best interest to end my days physically exhausted. When I returned to school the following fall, I continued this practice. It was one of the best things I have ever done for myself.

Being physically active will help you. Directing a portion of your energy toward athletics is good for you, and the more often that you can do it the better. After working out I can relax, and I am capable of concentrating on any task in front of me.

Exercise boosts Serotonin levels in your brain, making you happier. Exercise increases blood flow into your brain, leading to a sharper and more alert mind. Exercise at the end of a long day when your mind is tired but your body is not, and you will use up that extra energy, leading to better sleep. Exercise also keeps you healthy, and all of that other shit people are always telling you about.[35]

I'm not talking about a five-minute jog. I'm telling you to work out hard, and then see if it helps you regulate your physical and mental peaks and valleys. Now, I don't know if this has been scientifically proven, but it seems to help me.

A normal day for me has many different peaks, both physically and mentally. There are times when I cannot concentrate, because my mind seems to be going too fast, times when I can't shut up, and times when I absolutely cannot sit still. I go through each one of these different stages continuously, it seems. Sometimes it's awful, and sometimes it's not. When I work out, swim, box, ride my bicycle, or run hard for a couple of hours a day, these peaks become less extreme and less frequent. It is as if I am able to delay some of my energy until my workouts.

Another lesson that I learned from boxing was that I had the ability to set and reach goals. Before boxing, my goals were few and far between. Whenever I had previously tried to set goals, I got distracted and quit. And I justified my quitting by telling myself that the goals were unreasonable in the first place, and that I'd be better served embarking in a new direction.

---

35 And yes, I just started every sentence in this paragraph with the word "exercise."

But boxing was an all-or-none type of goal. If I didn't follow through on every aspect of training I wouldn't just lose, I would literally get my face beaten. So, I set the goal that I would win an amateur title. I worked hard, I made sacrifices, and I won a title in July of 2005, and I finished 3rd place in an international tournament later that August.

All of my hard work and training had paid off – the countless hours at the gym, the many miles run, the two concussions and bruised ribs – but I had reached my goal. I had what I believe alcoholics would call 'a moment of clarity'. I realized I could excel in one of the hardest sports in existence, so why couldn't I excel in college? There was no reason I couldn't.

Athletics are fulfilling. You learn a lot about yourself when you push your mind and body. You learn how far you are willing to go, and how much pain you can take. You'll discover that you can push harder, run faster, and you will learn something about yourself. You will be healthier, you will be sharper, and you will sleep better. And at the end of the day, you will see that pushing yourself, no matter what the task, will spread to other areas of your life.

ADHD medications: do you need meds?

Medication needs to be discussed, because it is such a prevalent aspect of our society. From talking with friends and members of the ADHD group over the years, it's become clear that different medications work for different people. What turns me into a senseless zombie and makes me stare at walls may be the exact medication that you need. And what makes your heart beat too fast and palms clammy might be the perfect amount for Josh. Who's Josh? I don't know, but that's the amount that he uses.

I have been prescribed Concerta, Ritalin, and Adderal. My

favorite of these was Adderal, because it worked the best for me.

In high school I was prescribed 56 milligrams of Concerta per day, and the side effects were horrible. It affected my appetite so drastically that in a three-month period I lost 15 to 20 pounds. Not only did I not feel hungry, at times I felt as though I would hurl if I tried to eat. Concerta also affected my personality.[36] I was spaced out all the time, and I remember my friends asking me what the hell was wrong with me. I got off Concerta after a few years. I'm still not sure why it took me so long to switch.

The next drug I was prescribed was Ritalin, and it worked much better for me. I was taking 20 milligrams of Ritalin, twice a day. Ritalin helped me focus well, and I didn't lose a drastic amount of weight. It also didn't turn me into a zombie. However, it made my hands uncomfortably sweaty, and sometimes it would make my heart beat ridiculously fast. When you are trying to read a textbook or pay attention in class, the last thing that you want is your heart racing at 120 beats per minute. I was on Ritalin for two years.

After the Ritalin, I was prescribed Adderal, and it was, by leaps and bounds, the best match for me. I took 20 milligrams, time-release (XR) every morning when I got up. I liked time-release much better than regular Adderal. Adderal didn't make my heart beat fast, my appetite and weight stayed constant, and there were no noticeable changes in my personality. It helped me focus, and it gave me the feeling that I was in control. I took Adderal for about six years.

There are many different medications for ADHD out there. Ritalin, Metadate, Concerta, Dexedrine, Vyvanse, Strattera, and Desoxyn. I have friends who tell me to try this or that new drug, but I was always happy with the Adderal. It seemed to help me, and I took it regularly.

ADHD medications shouldn't change who you are, or

---

36 Personality is pretty much all I've got going for me.

how you feel. Be aware of the cost-benefit ratio. Do you feel like shit on them? Do they make you unhappy? If they have negative side effects, think about switching to a different medication – if you are on medication in the first place. If you are not currently taking medication, or have never taken meds, consider what is going on in your life before you make a decision to try medications. Are you in school? Do you have problems concentrating in class or staying focused on homework? Do you have a job that requires you to be still and focused? Consider asking your doctor about trying medication. You need a reason to consider medication. Troubles with school and work, as well as day-to-day living are good reasons to consider medication, but if you think your current life wouldn't benefit from medication then keep on living without it.

ADHD medications should help you focus. If they do this, they are doing their job. They will not fix your life, do your homework for you, nor will they clean your room and do the dishes. Medications are not the be-all and end-all of managing ADHD. They are, simply, another small piece of the puzzle that works when used in conjunction with other techniques.

What else is going on?

People have asked me, "Why can't you just buckle down, and get your ADHD under control?" I just tell them it doesn't feel that simple. An important part of this process is understanding individually what each of us is facing in addition to ADHD, and then dealing with those problems accordingly.

ADHD has a high occurrence rate with other issues. Anxiety, depression, bi-polar, addiction and substance abuse, obsessive-compulsive disorder, and conduct disorders. So I ask you, what other problems are you facing?

If you are depressed, for example, organizational or study techniques are probably pretty low on the "to-do" list. As I've said before, I don't know what is happening in your life, so I can only tell you about what I have dealt with in my own life.

I have had three bouts of depression in my life. Although I never went to a doctor for them, I know what the black hole is like. I have seen the bottom of the bottle while trying to cope, I have slept through entire days, I have wondered how long it would last, and I have recovered.

I have been arrested three times, been questioned by the police a couple of dozen times, have a terrible driving record, have been in more fights than I care to mention, and I have the worst temper of anyone I know. I have been fired from a handful of jobs and also told a few bosses to go fuck themselves. To put it bluntly, I have some issues with authority and following rules/laws.

Last but not least, I have some minor problems with addiction and substance abuse. I have been to three court-ordered outpatient treatment programs for alcohol-related tickets. And I smoked a lot of weed every day for the better part of a decade.[37]

I am lucky. I have somehow managed to avoid prison, a serious drug habit, and death.[38] I have actually accomplished quite a bit of good as well – so far, so good.

I am not you, and I don't have a clue what your problems are, hell, you may not even have any. I am aware, however, that it is hard to tackle more than one large problem at a time.

When I was younger I had a psychiatrist who tried helping me, for about six or seven years, with anger management and other problems. At the age of 13 or 14, I started smoking weed, and I discovered that I wasn't so angry anymore.

---

37 I found that smoking weed also calmed my mind and helped damp down my energy levels.

38 "What do you want, a cookie?"

This was the cure for the moment, I think. I had to figure out the anger thing first, because I was imploding emotionally and there was no end in sight. When I started smoking weed, many of the things that would light the fuse started rolling off my shoulders. It gave me a new perspective, and I became less angry on a day-to-day basis. I had, for the moment, managed to quell my anger. It also relaxed me, and allowed me to slow down a bit.

I don't think it is possible to fix all of your problems at once. I'm trying to be realistic. Figuring out one or two issues at a time, actually making a change, and actually sustaining that change is a hard thing to do. If you want to succeed in school, at your job, or in a relationship, then you need to take a look at the other things that are making your life hard.

If you always feel better after talking to your parents, siblings, or friends, then by all means, talk away. But if you are suffering from serious bouts of depression or anxiety, you are having uncontrolled manic episodes, or you black out every time you get angry (my personal favorite), then you should talk to a professional. A therapist or counselor may not be exactly what you are looking for, but they can be helpful.

You will not be successful in the areas that you want to succeed in until you are successful in the areas that you need to succeed in. If your life is in shambles, because you are constantly getting high, every time you walk outside of your house you have a panic attack, or you spend the first half of every day organizing your shoes until they are "just right," then how do you expect to succeed in school, a job, or a relationship?

Figure it out.

Take care of yourself.

You can do it, but you have to be honest with yourself. Some questions to get you started:

- Am I currently happy?
- If I needed to change one thing about how my day went today, what would it be?
- Am I smoking way too much weed?
- Am I drinking too much?
- Am I playing video games or watching TV too often?
- How is my physical health?
- How is my mental health?
- Every time I see ______, I want to punch him/her in the face.[39]
- My job makes me ______.
- I wish I could ______.
- Every time I hang around ______, I feel happy and good.[40]
- I have always enjoyed ______.[41]
- Have I been doing things I want to, or am I doing things that other people want?

Although not an extensive list, questions like these are meant to increase self-awareness. If this list helps, great, if not, sit and write a list of your own, or talk with someone, or look online. It doesn't matter what you do, but you need to look within yourself and decide what issues you need to address. To understand what you need to do, you have to look at yourself honestly.

It is important that we deal with the issues that are by-products of ADHD, but we have to deal with the most important issues first. I don't care what people say about the

39 Spend less time around this person.
40 Spend more time around this person.
41 Do this activity more often.

importance of list-making as it relates to time-management, if you are at the bottom of a bottle of Jack Daniels, for whatever the reason, that list can probably wait.

In the ADHD support group at MSU, I heard many different stories about personal struggles. A large majority of us are dealing with other issues, and we need to address them. There is no shame in the matter, it is just a fact of life, and it is different for each of us. Please, take care of yourself.

Breaking habitual procrastination

I find there are two main types of procrastination: successful procrastination and habitual procrastination. Both types are comprised of different attributes, and, although not always mutually exclusive, there is a line that separates them. Let me begin by defining what I see as the two types of procrastination.

Successful procrastination involves putting things off but still getting them done. You have all week to write a paper, or all day to go to the drug store and get a prescription filled for grandma, and you put it off until the last minute: you start your paper the night before it's due, and you get to the drugstore five minutes before it closes. I call this successful, because, although you delayed doing them, you still managed to get them done. You can live with this type of procrastination. The paper may have been only a rough draft, and grandma might be receiving her meds a little late at night, but they got done. Way to go. The question that you have to ask yourself when you "successfully procrastinate" is, how much has your procrastination affected the quality of the end product?

Habitual procrastination involves not getting anything done, repeatedly. You have a month to write a research paper, half a semester to do a project, or six weeks to call the courthouse, and you don't do anything. You have failed. You have done nothing. "Oh well," you say, "it wasn't that important anyway."

Habitual procrastination is not okay. It can cause serious problems with school, work, and relationships (and the list goes on). This is the type of procrastination that we need to focus on. This is the type that we need to stop doing. So how do we fix this problem? First, let's look at the different thought processes that lead us to procrastination.

Ways that I procrastinate:

(A) I forget to do something. Either because I haven't written it down or it didn't seem too important, I have allowed it to slip my mind. This leads to less time to get it done (if I remember it) or to missing a deadline (if I don't remember it).

(B) I get distracted from the task at hand. As I am about to get started on a task, I get interrupted/distracted and do something else. Or I may start something, and then after a bit simply stop working on it and feel like I have "done enough."

(C) I put it off. I delay. I don't want to start the task or face the music (so to speak). When this happens, I am an active participant in this act (to be explained further).

(D) I avoid the task at hand. This may be due to anxiety or reasons such as making up foregone conclusions (e.g., "I'm going to fail this class anyways, so what's the point of studying for this final).

(E) I lie to myself about the importance of the task. This not only diminishes the likelihood that I attempt the task, by steering it further down the mental to-do list, it allows me to completely disregard it as something that needs getting done at all.

So how do we stop habitual procrastination?

I have broken it down into four parts:

- Pack as much as possible into your day.
- Add simple tasks to your daily routine.
- Break the habit and change behavior.
- The time-limit theory.

I spoke previously about the benefits of packing as much as possible into your daily routine, and I come back to it here. Filling your day creates a sense of urgency. You have many things to do and many places to be. The larger number of tasks that you are trying to complete and the sense of urgency that accompanies your packed day leads to accomplishing more. When you operate at this higher capacity, getting things done becomes almost automatic – you don't have time to think about doing things, you just get them done.

Adding simple tasks to your daily routine – no matter how mundane – such as doing the dishes, vacuuming, laundry, etc., gets you in the habit of being productive and allows you to win many smaller battles. You are doing things without putting them off, and this can become contagious to other activities.

Breaking the habit and changing behavior is the hardest part to accomplish. Habitual procrastination happens both actively and passively, so it must be dealt with in two different ways.

As a passive participant (A & B), you must put yourself in the best position to stop forgetting to do something, or becoming distracted from a task, by altering your routines to minimize the opportunities for either to happen. Write things down so you don't forget them. Shut your phone off and disconnect your computer so you don't get distracted from doing a reading assignment. Forgetting to do something and becoming distracted from a task are things that happen without your being aware of it. You need to alter your routine to include "safety-nets" that minimize the possibilities of these occurring.

As an active participant (C, D, & E) you must become aware of the moments in which you participate in the act – putting something off until later, avoiding something, or lying to yourself. Then, after catching yourself in the act of becoming an active participant in the habitual procrastination, you have to learn to stop your mind, catch it doing wrong, and try and change that behavior. You need to, effectively, catch yourself reaching into the cookie jar, and then cut your own hand off. This is not easy.

A favorite way that experts say to stave off procrastination is by setting yourself a time limit of sorts and then starting your task. This would sound something like, "I'm going to read the paper for five minutes, and then I'm going to start my homework." This is similar to my crossword puzzle as part of my warm-up in the "Study Routines" section. An effective technique when used at certain times, but it's limited in its effectiveness. With all the different ways to procrastinate, how could this possibly be a solution to everything? It can't be, because it only addresses the postponing or delaying of a task. Therefore, it can only be useful part of the time.

When you are trying to get things accomplished it is best to keep your mouth shut about it. Don't tell others. Don't even say it out loud. It has to do with feeling like you have accomplished something by simply saying it. This seems relevant in a specific area, namely, when you are telling a friend about how much work you have to do, and you start going into specifics, and then you tell four other people, after a while it seems as if you have accomplished half of the task, because you have spent so much time talking about it. So keep your mouth shut.

A work environment (i.e., an office or work area) can negate some of the powers of procrastination. If you need to get work done, and everything that you need for the work is in that room/office, then simply walking into that room and sitting down accounts for roughly three-quarters of the battle. One minute you are outside of the room, and the next you are at a desk. Office mode. Your environment has gone from one with a TV or a couch as its focal point, to one that is geared towards work. Put yourself in a position to win with office mode.

Procrastination. It's a bastard, no doubt about it. But you can be successful in dealing with it – in changing behavior and in being honest with yourself. Understanding why you do what you do can only lead to improvement.

Instant gratification

"Daaaaad, can I open my presents yet?"
"No. It's not Christmas. You have to wait until the morning."
"What about just one?"
"No."
"Can I just hold one? Let me just hold one."
"No."
"Come on dad. I can't even just hold one? What's the big deal? I'm not gonna open it."
"You have to wait until the morning."
"Pleaaaaaaaaaase. Puh-leeeeeeeeeease."
"No. Ugh. Ask your mother."
"Mommmmmm. Can I open just one present tonight?"
"What did your dad say?"
"He said 'maybe'?"
"That's a lie. I said no."
"You guys are unfair, and it's clear you hate me."

The night before Christmas, running around in circles trying to tear into the first gift – exactly who I am.

Waiting for stuff sucks, let's face it. But sometimes it's a good idea to be patient, or at least, to try to be patient. I am impatient, and I am constantly seeking out things that instantly gratify. I've heard that this is a generational trait, a result of the baby boomers parenting, but who knows.

When I was younger this need for gratification manifested itself in the pursuit of adrenaline highs such as skateboarding, BMX, climbing and jumping off things, and getting into fistfights. A few years down the road this energy was focused into boxing, and then a pack-a-day cigarette habit. And now, I'm hooked on autoerotic asphyxiation.[42]

What I know about instant gratification is that sometimes you have to embrace it, and sometimes you have to shut it down.

It's a nice day outside, the sun is shining, and there are people playing basketball on the court a block down from your house. You really want to go play basketball. It's all you can think about. Actually, you're thinking about playing basketball so much that you are getting absolutely zero schoolwork done. You are wasting time. Go play. Just walk away, go outside, and play. Then, when you are finished, come back in and do some work. You do what you want to, so that you can come back later and do what you have to.

There are times, however, when you must delay gratification, and I am not only referring to scholarly pursuits.

When you have already been warned about showing up to work high, then it is not a good idea to smoke weed five minutes before the start of your shift. If you have $2,000 worth of credit card debt, well, you might want to reconsider buying that new $1,500 flat-screen TV. If you really want to make out with that girl at the bar while your girlfriend is in the bathroom, then you'd better be prepared for the consequences.

One of the best tricks I have learned is simply being aware of when I will be able to delay and when I won't.

---

42 I have never actually tried autoerotic asphyxiation.

When you are on an extreme energy kick,[43] you can't shut up, your mind is racing, or you really want to do something – go swimming, driving, go to the store, shoot a gun – well, these are times when it is a good idea to simply go ahead and keep on being you. Trying to convince yourself that you are not all over the place, and delaying gratification, is some square-peg/round-hole stuff. It just doesn't work.

You have to pick out the spots when things, both in your mind and body, are a little calmer. Haven't eaten all day, and all you can think about is food? Guess what? You probably won't be having a successful study session. Go eat, and then study. When necessary, get the urge out of the way, and then you'll be able to concentrate on the task at hand.

For me, the need for instant gratification is mainly a problem when it interferes with or diverts me from an ongoing task. Which is why I suggest appeasing any wants prior to studying. Sometimes, though, you have to struggle through and completely ignore any and all impulses.

You are sitting in your room, studying for a big exam the next morning, and your friend, who you haven't seen in a month, calls you and asks if you want to go to a party with four girls and him. But, your entire semester is riding on this exam grade. Well, my friend, you have got to shut it down.[44] You have to actively sit there, pull the phone away from your face, look at it for three to six seconds, and tell your friend and the four sex-starved co-eds that, unfortunately, you just can't swing it tonight. You have to convince yourself, regardless of the fact that you haven't been laid in four months, that it is not a good idea to go party with a bunch of hot girls and your best friend. Life is shit, I know. But, learning how to delay gratification will enable you to experience control, and this feeling is an important one to know. This fleeting feeling of control leads us to our next topic.

---

43 ADHD supreme. AKA: The majority of my life.

44 You could turn off your phone at such a crucial time, but I don't want to ask too much of you.

Learning when to say "yes" and when to say "no"

I am not a good decision maker. I prefer to go with whims and gut feelings – less thinking, more doing. I really can't recall making decisions before the age of 19. Actually spending time to consider and weigh options is not one of my strong suits. Regardless of actually making "good" decisions, the idea is to make a decision within the context of the situation you are in – the right decision at the right time. Yes or no.

Going from place-to-place and activity-to-activity is good, if you have it mapped out. Without this map, life becomes chaotic – a state of being that I am sure you are familiar with. I spent many years quite content not knowing what I was going to do next, acting on whims, and living without structure. Although fun, this type of living leads to severe mediocrity in the collegiate world.[45]

And so, I ask you: How good are you at saying yes and no? Do you know? Are you aware of situations you have experienced when you've been able to summon up the power to say no? Making the simplest yes/no decision provides you with a different type of freedom (about which I spoke in the previous section): the freedom of self-control. Knowing this feeling is pretty amazing.

My world moves very quickly, internally and externally. Taking the time to actually think about a decision before making it is something that I am naturally uncomfortable with. On the surface this hardly looks like a problem, but when you get deeper it becomes a trap. Giving in to whims and reacting to everything, instead of deciding, is an existence without choice. Self-control enables you to think things through before making decisions. Self-control leads

---

45 Some people get through college with minimal effort and mediocre grades just fine. Personally, after two years of mediocrity I was ready to drop out.

to a new level of freedom.

You cannot be successful at something without working at it. And you cannot find time to work at it if you cannot say no – no to yourself, and no to others.

People need things from you, people want to spend time with you, and bosses want you to come in early or pick up an extra shift. Without being an asshole, embrace the power of saying no. Use it appropriately, when you know that you have something else more important to do.

Picture this on a large scale – you'll have more time to do the things you want or need to do, because you can say "no" to your whims, "no" to wasting time, and "no" to unimportant solicitations for your time. Getting comfortable using the word "no" will help you better regulate your whims and impulsiveness. Saying "no" may not regulate all of your impulses, but it will help you regulate those options presented to you by others – the trivial or untimely requests to attend a party or help someone move, go to the movies, or eat at a restaurant. If you don't have time, you don't have time. Say no. And then spend that time doing what you need to do for school, work, or yourself.

Reasonable expectations

There are no limitations to the things we can do, the amount of money that we can make, the success we can have in our relationships, or anything else. In identifying problem areas, breaking habits, making behavioral changes, creating routines that work, dealing with stressors, and learning how to operate at a higher and more efficient capacity, we need to understand that there is no quick fix and this is not a short battle.

It would be ridiculous for any person to make a few dozen giant lifestyle changes within one, two, or even three years.

Making a lasting change takes time. Identifying your problem areas – not problems, as in, something is wrong with you, but rather something is not working for you – means that you have done something that many people never do: you have been honest with yourself. Understand that you can make a significant, overall change by simply making small changes in the right direction.

One of the smallest changes I ever made had an enormous impact on my scholastic career. I bought a pen. I am not joking. I bought a Pilot ExecuGel, and it was everything that I needed in a pen – it had great weight, it was comfortable in my grip, it was aesthetically pleasing, and, most importantly, it improved my handwriting immensely. Because of this pen, taking notes became more tolerable. The ink was a dark black that seemed to pop off the page, and this made reading my notes easier.

This pen transformed my understanding of what I could do to improve my experience in college. The things I had control over and could change, no matter the size, could have a giant impact. Because of this pen, I began looking at my life, both in and out of the classroom, to see what else I could alter. Right now, ask yourself: What other things can I do? Refrain from asking, "What other things should I do?" You should do whatever it is that you can do, first. Find your weaknesses and start chipping away at them. These things will take time – we are trying to make life changes not quick fixes. What is clear to me now, and I hope will become clear to you too, is this: any amount of change in the right direction, no matter how small, is better than no change at all.

Trial and error

The best thing you can do is to learn what works for you and what doesn't. I learn best via trial and error. When I was ten, an eight-year-old cut off my left index finger with a pair of garden shears. Okay, not off-off, but off enough that it was only hanging by some skin and half a bone, and I required around four hours of microsurgery to put it back together. Guess what? Since that incident I have never had another injury involving an eight-year-old with garden shears. Lesson learned? I think so.

Trial and error is the perfect guide on the journey toward self-improvement. Having a curious and introspective attitude, accompanied by the wherewithal to embrace the trial and error method of life, will help you overcome a lot of the issues related to ADHD.

The more curious you are, the better. You want to know what works for you? And you want to try those things out? Then, my friend, you cannot fail. You will gain knowledge of self by discovering what works and what is garbage.

You must attempt something. It can be a tip or suggestion that I am writing about, something you read on the Internet or heard on the radio, something a friend told you, or something from another book. You don't have to tell anybody about the changes you are trying to make. Your successes and failures are only yours to know. Just try anything. If it is a success, great, if not, say fuck it, remember that that particular technique doesn't work for you, and move on. Then repeat the process.

Everyone is different

This is self-explanatory, really, but just in case it needs further clarification, here it goes. As psychological and physiological beings, we are all different.[46] Isn't that great? And because of this fact, I have made an effort to repeatedly state

46 Yes, Tyler Durden would disagree.

the obvious: I am not you, and you are not me.

We may have some common traits, attitudes, beliefs, or struggles and successes, and I have tried to highlight these. However, we also differ in a myriad of ways. We've had different upbringings. We have different psychological makeups, life experiences, personal strengths and weaknesses, and a different physiology.

So, when medication doesn't work the same for you as it does for your friend, remember, he is different than you. He may metabolize it slower or faster. The drug may have a greater efficacy in his system than yours. You are different. In the same way that reading notes aloud may be the only thing that works for you, a friend of yours might think it the dumbest thing he has ever heard. So be it, you are different.

This is a world of standardized testing – ACTs, SATs, MCATs, GREs, GMATs, CATs, MEAPs – predetermined curriculums, standardized procedures, and other attempts to lump people together into groups or create "norms" by which everybody learns. And because of all this garbage, you must take the helm of your own intellectual ship. You do this by looking at the current system and seeing where it is failing you, and deciding what needs changing. And then, you try to make those changes.

Remember, nothing is wrong with you. You are awesome. I don't even know you, but I know I am awesome, and I have ADHD, so if you have ADHD, by the transitive property,[47] you are also awesome. But remember, although we share a certain amount of awesomeness, we are different. Everyone is.

47 A=B, B=C, so A=C. D=cupcakes.

Passions

Do you feel drawn to something? Do it, whatever it may be. The best way to enjoy learning is to learn about things you have a passion for. Continue learning about it, do the work, become an expert, and then get paid to do what you are passionate about. Okay, even if you don't get paid, simply doing things that you are passionate about is an extremely close second.

Major in a subject that you are passionate about, and college will become easier. It will be easier because you will enjoy what you are doing. The opposite side of the spectrum being, you hate your job, and going to work is dreadful – everybody has been there at least once. If you are wondering what you are going to do in school or work in the future, take a look at what you are passionate about. Now.

I would trade in all the gadgets, smart phones, and flat screens for a chance to do things that I am passionate about.[48] And, in the sage words of an ex-boss of mine, "If you can't get paid for doing something that you're passionate about, then you should at least do something [for work] that allows you enough free-time to do that thing."

It comes down to priorities, so get your ducks in order. If you are currently in school, or you are going to be in school soon, or you are thinking about going back to school – school of any kind – I ask you, what is holding you back from succeeding? You can learn anything you want to. So, why aren't you? If you start doing something you love, and you put forth effort and persistence, then you will be successful at it. I promise.

48 I don't own anything cool.

Acknowledgments

This book would have remained a pile of papers in my room without the help of Josh Izenberg and Alex Pappas.

Mom, Pops, Max Owen, Jamie Killen, Adam Schlecte, Kristine Mudd, Bob Dargel, Rochelle Flumenbaum, and Alex Bentz. Thank you for your involvement, support, and wisdom along the way.

About the Author

Phill Pappas is currently doing laundry.
He lives in Austin, Texas where he writes and performs.

Made in the USA
San Bernardino, CA
10 November 2015